Hal•Leonard
INSTRUMENTAL PLAY-ALONG

TENOR SAX

WOMEN OF POP

How To Use The CD Accompaniment:

A melody cue appears on the right channel only.
If your CD player has a balance adjustment, you can adjust the volume
of the melody by turning down the right channel.

The CD is playable on any CD player, and is also enhanced so Mac and PC users
can adjust the recording to any tempo without changing the pitch!

ISBN: 978-1-4584-2033-6

HAL•LEONARD®
CORPORATION

7777 W. BLUEMOUND RD. P.O. BOX 13819 MILWAUKEE, WI 53213

Visit Hal Leonard Online at
www.halleonard.com

T0019748

CONTENTS

4

BAD ROMANCE

TENOR SAX

Words and Music by
STEFANI GERMANOTTA and NADIR KHAYAT

5

CHASING PAVEMENTS

TENOR SAX

Words and Music by
ADELE ADKINS and FRANCIS EG WHITE

THE EDGE OF GLORY

3

TENOR SAX

Words and Music by STEFANI GERMANOTTA,
PAUL BLAIR and FERNANDO GARIBAY

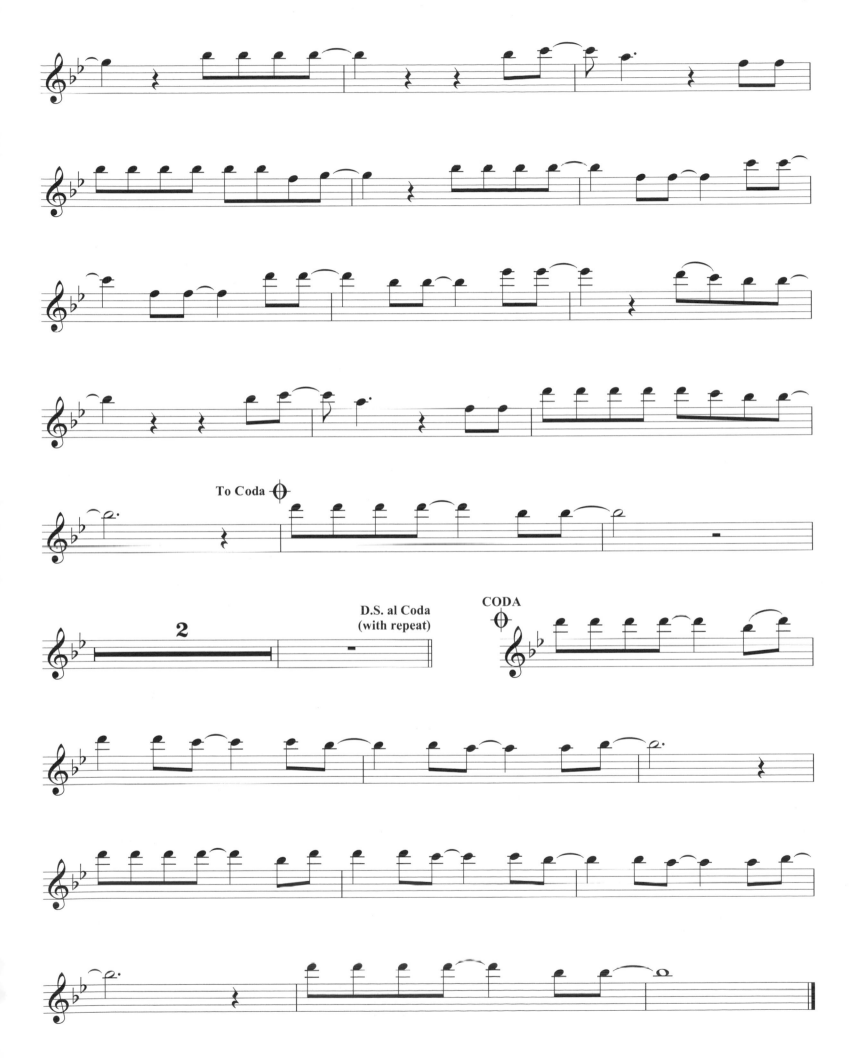

FALLIN' FOR YOU

4

TENOR SAX

Words and Music by
COLBIE CAILLAT and RICK NOWELS

JAR OF HEARTS

TENOR SAX

Words and Music by BARRETT YERETSIAN,
CHRISTINA PERRI and DREW LAWRENCE

Slowly, with feeling

rit.   *p*

LAST FRIDAY NIGHT (T.G.I.F.)

TENOR SAX

Words and Music by LUKASZ GOTTWALD,
MAX MARTIN, BONNIE McKEE and KATY PERRY

KING OF ANYTHING

TENOR SAX

Words and Music by
SARA BAREILLES

MEAN

TENOR SAX

Words and Music by
TAYLOR SWIFT

Moderately

MY LIFE WOULD SUCK WITHOUT YOU

TENOR SAX

Words and Music by LUKASZ GOTTWALD,
MAX MARTIN and CLAUDE KELLY

RAISE YOUR GLASS

TENOR SAX

Words and Music by ALECIA MOORE,
MAX MARTIN and JOHAN SCHUSTER

OUR SONG

TENOR SAX

Words and Music by
TAYLOR SWIFT

ROLLING IN THE DEEP

Words and Music by
ADELE ADKINS and PAUL EPWORTH

TENOR SAX

SINGLE LADIES
(Put a Ring on It)

TENOR SAX

Words and Music by BEYONCE KNOWLES,
THADDIS HARRELL, CHRISTOPHER STEWART and TERIUS NASH

TEENAGE DREAM

TENOR SAX

Words and Music by LUKASZ GOTTWALD, MAX MARTIN,
BENJAMIN LEVIN, BONNIE McKEE and KATY PERRY

WHAT THE HELL

Words and Music by AVRIL LAVIGNE,
MAX MARTIN and JOHAN SCHUSTER

TENOR SAX

HAL•LEONARD INSTRUMENTAL PLAY-ALONG

Your favorite songs are arranged just for solo instrumentalists with this outstanding series. Each book includes a great full-accompaniment play-along CD so you can sound just like a pro! Check out www.halleonard.com to see all the titles available.

Disney Greats

Arabian Nights • Hawaiian Roller Coaster Ride • It's a Small World • Look Through My Eyes • Yo Ho (A Pirate's Life for Me) • and more.

_____ 00841934	Flute	$12.95
_____ 00841935	Clarinet	$12.95
_____ 00841936	Alto Sax	$12.95
_____ 00841937	Tenor Sax	$12.95
_____ 00841938	Trumpet	$12.95
_____ 00841939	Horn	$12.95
_____ 00841940	Trombone	$12.95
_____ 00841941	Violin	$12.95
_____ 00841942	Viola	$12.95
_____ 00841943	Cello	$12.95
_____ 00842078	Oboe	$12.95

Glee

And I Am Telling You I'm Not Going • Defying Gravity • Don't Stop Believin' • Keep Holding On • Lean on Me • No Air • Sweet Caroline • True Colors • and more.

_____ 00842479	Flute	$12.99
_____ 00842480	Clarinet	$12.99
_____ 00842481	Alto Sax	$12.99
_____ 00842482	Tenor Sax	$12.99
_____ 00842483	Trumpet	$12.99
_____ 00842484	Horn	$12.99
_____ 00842485	Trombone	$12.99
_____ 00842486	Violin	$12.99
_____ 00842487	Viola	$12.99
_____ 00842488	Cello	$12.99

Movie Music

And All That Jazz • Come What May • I Am a Man of Constant Sorrow • I Walk the Line • Seasons of Love • Theme from Spider Man • and more.

_____ 00842089	Flute	$10.95
_____ 00842090	Clarinet	$10.95
_____ 00842091	Alto Sax	$10.95
_____ 00842092	Tenor Sax	$10.95
_____ 00842093	Trumpet	$10.95
_____ 00842094	Horn	$10.95
_____ 00842095	Trombone	$10.95
_____ 00842096	Violin	$10.95
_____ 00842097	Viola	$10.95
_____ 00842098	Cello	$10.95

Elvis Presley

All Shook Up • Blue Suede Shoes • Can't Help Falling in Love • Don't Be Cruel • Hound Dog • Jailhouse Rock • Love Me Tender • Return to Sender • and more.

_____ 00842363	Flute	$12.99
_____ 00842367	Trumpet	$12.99
_____ 00842368	Horn	$12.99
_____ 00842369	Trombone	$12.99
_____ 00842370	Violin	$12.99
_____ 00842371	Viola	$12.99
_____ 00842372	Cello	$12.99

Sports Rock

Another One Bites the Dust • Centerfold • Crazy Train • Get Down Tonight • Let's Get It Started • Shout • The Way You Move • and more.

_____ 00842326	Flute	$12.99
_____ 00842327	Clarinet	$12.99
_____ 00842328	Alto Sax	$12.99
_____ 00842329	Tenor Sax	$12.99
_____ 00842330	Trumpet	$12.99
_____ 00842331	Horn	$12.99
_____ 00842332	Trombone	$12.99
_____ 00842333	Violin	$12.99
_____ 00842334	Viola	$12.99
_____ 00842335	Cello	$12.99

TV Favorites

The Addams Family Theme • The Brady Bunch • Green Acres Theme • Happy Days • Johnny's Theme • Linus and Lucy • NFL on Fox Theme • Theme from the Simpsons • and more.

_____ 00842079	Flute	$10.95
_____ 00842080	Clarinet	$10.95
_____ 00842081	Alto Sax	$10.95
_____ 00842082	Tenor Sax	$10.95
_____ 00842083	Trumpet	$10.95
_____ 00842084	Horn	$10.95
_____ 00842085	Trombone	$10.95
_____ 00842086	Violin	$10.95
_____ 00842087	Viola	$10.95
_____ 00842088	Cello	$10.95

Twilight

Bella's Lullaby • Decode • Eyes on Fire • Full Moon • Go All the Way (Into the Twilight) • Leave Out All the Rest • Spotlight (Twilight Remix) • Supermassive Black Hole • Tremble for My Beloved.

_____ 00842406	Flute	$12.99
_____ 00842407	Clarinet	$12.99
_____ 00842408	Alto Sax	$12.99
_____ 00842409	Tenor Sax	$12.99
_____ 00842410	Trumpet	$12.99
_____ 00842411	Horn	$12.99
_____ 00842412	Trombone	$12.99
_____ 00842413	Violin	$12.99
_____ 00842414	Viola	$12.99
_____ 00842415	Cello	$12.99

Twilight – New Moon

Almost a Kiss • Dreamcatcher • Edward Leaves • I Need You • Memories of Edward • New Moon • Possibility • Roslyn • Satellite Heart • and more.

_____ 00842458	Flute	$12.99
_____ 00842459	Clarinet	$12.99
_____ 00842460	Alto Sax	$12.99
_____ 00842461	Tenor Sax	$12.99
_____ 00842462	Trumpet	$12.99
_____ 00842463	Horn	$12.99
_____ 00842464	Trombone	$12.99
_____ 00842465	Violin	$12.99
_____ 00842466	Viola	$12.99
_____ 00842467	Cello	$12.99

Wicked

As Long As You're Mine • Dancing Through Life • Defying Gravity • For Good • I'm Not That Girl • Popular • The Wizard and I • and more.

_____ 00842236	Book/CD Pack	$11.95
_____ 00842237	Book/CD Pack	$11.95
_____ 00842238	Alto Saxophone	$11.95
_____ 00842239	Tenor Saxophone	$11.95
_____ 00842240	Trumpet	$11.95
_____ 00842241	Horn	$11.95
_____ 00842242	Trombone	$11.95
_____ 00842243	Violin	$11.95
_____ 00842244	Viola	$11.95
_____ 00842245	Cello	$11.95

FOR MORE INFORMATION, SEE YOUR LOCAL MUSIC DEALER, OR WRITE TO:

HAL•LEONARD® CORPORATION
7777 W. BLUEMOUND RD. P.O. BOX 13819 MILWAUKEE, WI 53213